GROWING IN CHRIST

Oluwagbemiga Olowosoyo

ISBN 978-1-365-35741-1

1 Grand Street,
Bridgeport.
CT 06604
Tel: +12035053614, +12404423634

P. O. Box 36706,
Dugbe, Ibadan
Oyo State, Nigeria
Tel: +234(0)8034652119, +234(0)8056257056

E. Mail: olowosoyo@yahoo.com

Website: www.olowosoyo.org

Bible quotes are from the King James Version unless otherwise stated.

Contents

Dedication

I want to dedicate this book to

Gbolahan & Ine Olude

in whose home in Montreal I am putting finishing touches to this book.

Thanks for great assistance in the work God commissioned me to do in Canada.

Born of God

> *But as many as received Him, to them He gave the right to become children of God, to those who believe in His name:*
>
> *John 1:12*

I am bearing Olowosoyo because my father bears that name. He gave me the authority to bear that name. No one can stop me from bearing that name. I have every legal power to bear that name.

Since my father is a Nigerian, I am also a Nigerian. No one can stop me from being a Nigerian. This is what we call heritage.

Now, since I have the right to bear the name Olowosoyo, I also have the power to give birth to children and call them by that name.

Therefore, it will not be wrong to say, the son of Olowosoyo is Olowosoyo. That is how the family is maintained.

I was standing on the road once with my daughter. Then one of her colleagues in school was passing by. That one shouted Olowosoyo. And I thought she was calling me. But my girl was actually the one who responded. Initially, I felt embarrassed "who was this small girl shouting my name?" But when my daughter responded, I realised the small girl was right. My daughter had a legal right to answer the same name. Olowosoyo is my name. It is also her name.

> *But as many as received Him, to them He gave the right to become children of God, to those who believe in His name:*
>
> *John 1:12*

When a man hears the gospel, he receives the Word of God. You will remember that God is the Word.

> *In the beginning was the Word, and the Word was with God, and the Word was God.*
>
> *John 1:1*

God is the Word. Therefore, when a man hears the gospel, he has received a part of God. Better still, you can say he has received the seed of God, the Power of God.

When creation was done in Genesis chapter 1, it was completely by the Word of God. Therefore, it will not be out of place to call the Word of God, the seed (power of God).

The heart of man is like the womb of the woman. It receives the gospel, the seed of God.

When the heart responds to the gospel, we can say there was fertilisation or conception. However, there is no birth until that individual confesses the Lord Jesus with his mouth. And publicly declare his intention to be born again. And then we say he is a new creature.

> *Therefore, if anyone is in Christ, he is a new creation; old things have passed away; behold, all things have become new.*
>
> *2 Corinthians 5:17*

Just as a new-born baby, he is a new creature. He is completely new.

This new person is not just a human being; he is a combination of the seed of God and the egg of the human being. Therefore he is a god. He is not God. And he cannot be God. To be God, he couldn't have been born. He needed to exist from the beginning on his own. Also since man is involved, the product cannot be God. But since God's seed is involved, the product cannot be completely human. He is a god.

When a white man and a black woman are involved in sex and reproduction occurs, the child is neither black nor white. It is a half-caste. The same way the product of the Seed of God and the heart of man cannot be man, or God. He is a half-caste, a god.

The implication of this is serious. It means that the son has divine inheritance that cannot be removed.

> *In Him also we have obtained an inheritance, being predestined according to the purpose of Him who*

works all things according to the counsel of His will,

Ephesians 1:11

Just by that singular action of salvation, you have been born into the family of God. Not as a slave in the family but as a son and as an heir unto God.

That is great.

When a child is born into a wealthy family, everyone knows that it is a great thing. All the slaves celebrate it. Whether they like it or not, they must serve the son.

As a Son of God, you cannot beg for bread. You cannot suffer like any other person. All the strength of your father is made available to assist you, and establish you.

But you are a chosen generation, a royal priesthood, a holy nation, His own special people, that you may proclaim the praises of Him who called you out of darkness into His marvellous light;

Who once were not a people but are now the people of God, who had not obtained mercy but now have obtained mercy.

1 Peter 2:9-10

Understanding Growth

Text: Hebrews 5:12-14

Memory Verse: 1 Peter 2:1-2

Introduction

Growth is very important in the existence of living things. As a matter of fact, every living thing grows. It is a sign of life.

In Genesis, God instructed every living thing He made to grow and produce of its kind. Therefore, it is not just a pleasurable thing to grow, it is divine commandment.

In the scripture above, Paul was explaining that God is unhappy about a set of believers who gave their lives to Christ and have been in the faith for a while. They were expected to have grown but they were still babies in the faith.

How did he know? It is obvious because spiritual growth is very similar to physical growth. It could be measured.

Importance of spiritual growth

1. It brings joy to the parent: (in this case) God, who had invested so much to your growth.
2. It reduces the burden created for those God is using to disciple you. They will have no reason to be carrying you around as a baby, any longer.
3. It strengthens the body of Christ (Church). The church is made up of people and when each one is strong, the entire church is strong.
4. Creates a major problem for the kingdom of darkness, because a matured believer is light; terror to darkness. When light is so bright, there is no space for darkness.

5. You become less vulnerable to demonic incursion. In fact, he would be afraid of you.
6. You become a blessing to the world around you because you know what you need to know and you destroy the work of the devil around you.
7. You become a powerful, dependable instrument (worker) for God; helping to win and disciple others.
8. You are happy with yourself. Growth brings happiness.
9. If a believer is not growing, it is a sign of spiritual kwashiorkor (disease) because God would never fail on His part.
10. Failure to grow means you are a failure.

Prayer Points

1. Every living thing grows, I will grow!

2. Growth is a divine commandment therefore I will grow in faith.
3. The parent can only provide food. He can't compel food into the child. Help me to develop a zeal, thirst or strong desire to grow in faith.
4. Of course, my growth would be great problem for the devil. Therefore, it is obvious why he is trying to stop my growth.
   - Every effort of the devil to hinder my spiritual growth is hereby truncated.
5. Deliver me from spiritual Kwashiorkor.
6. God is expecting so much from my growth. I will not become a failure to Him.

Baby Believers

Text: 1 Corinthians 3:1-23

Introduction

This stage is very crucial in the life of every believer. As a matter of fact, it cannot be wished away.

This is the time when a believer had just accepted Jesus Christ. He does not fully understand what has happened to him/her; except of course, that he is saved.

Just like a baby can't be left to him/herself, this period is characterized by much of dependence. And the person playing the role of discipler would have much to do at that time.

One of the worst traits of the baby Christian is that he/she is very selfish. He thinks only of himself and his interest. And if his needs are not met immediately, he fights. This manifests in all things: his prayer points, his interests, the way he manages his time and resources, etc.

His ego is very sharp. He still has strong interests in things of the world he claims to have left behind. There is almost no way to convince him to give his resources to God or to serve.

How to Grow

1. Growth takes conscious rigorous efforts.
2. Desire the Milk of the Word of God.
    a) Be excited to be in fellowship where you will hear and absorb the word of God.
    b) Read literature materials that simplify the Word of God.
    c) Listen and watch the movies of the teaching of the Word of God.
    d) Read the Bible personally, daily and take notes from it.

e) Meditate on what you read or discover in the Bible.

3. Being confused about what you study in the Word is a sign that you are doing well.
4. Bring up your questions, confusions, and disagreements to your discipler or the leaders.
5. Make it a habit to follow or obey everything you discover in the Bible.
6. Follow the ten principles of establishment in the faith. (Determination, personal relationship with God, change your friends, separation, commitment to fellowship, bold declaration of faith, take God's word serious, throw away the sin, readiness to make sacrifice, and get busy in His work).

Conclusion

If you pay attention to these points you will grow naturally from babyhood. Meanwhile, each individual's pace is his/her prerogative. That is, your seriousness or otherwise decides your growth pace. And that is the reason why several believers fail to grow.

Prayer Points

1. I am glad that I am your baby, oh God! But I must not remain a spiritual baby for ever.
   - Lord, move me forward in my faith.
2. Help me to develop a strong desire for growth.
3. Let your Holy Spirit help to coordinate my spiritual growth.
4. I have been a burden on others for too long. It is time for me to become a blessing to others.
   - Deliver me from a commitment to self and the flesh.

5. Take me through every experience that would mature me as a believer.
6. I have become an old baby Christian. I need you to jump-start my growth from babyhood.
7. Quicken my babyhood stage.

Young Believers

Text: 1 Corinthians 4:1-3

Introduction

Just as it implies, this is the stage immediately after babyhood. The believer is still young but he is no longer a baby.

Just like it had been said in previous studies, it is not a function of time, but choices and commitment. In essence, the number of years in the faith is not the major subject but commitment.

The young believer may not hold anyone to ransom, but he still depends on others for almost everything.

They are the believers who can't take the pain to determine the will of God, and would be following prophets around. They are more eager to enjoy the miraculous than to judge by what spirit it is done.

The strong tendency about the young believers is that they easily get carried away by carnal things that easily mix with spiritual. For example, they love titles more than service. They enjoy the praise of men than pleasing God.

They fast and pray just to boast and not necessarily to seek God. They read the Bible, not because they love God, but because they want to identify, and enjoy the blessings therein. They give offerings to God because of what they stand to gain, or because they would benefit in the purpose of giving.

How To Grow

1. Take conscious efforts to develop yourself through topical, character and book studies in the word of God. That is, you go beyond just normal 30 minutes quiet time of reading one chapter a day or using materials like Daily Guide; every time.

2. Whether you have the opportunity to preach or not, develop study outlines of your own and write them out in your note.
3. Raise or participate in Bible discussion groups, particularly practical discussion (Sunday school) house fellowships, etc.
4. Don't fight when you are criticized, or spoken against. In fact you should be glad, because it helps to destroy your ego and self-conceit.
5. Pummel your body through consistent fasting and prayers (personal and joint).
6. Do less of praying for yourself (that is a proof of your faith in God) but for others in organized serious intercession.
7. Jump at every opportunity to take part in God's work, particularly sharing your faith with others.
8. Shift your attention from men, their praise, their errors, etc.; and set your love, focus and attention on God.

9. Learn to be led (through continuous relationship) by the Spirit of God.
10. Seek to know God, and not your benefits.

Conclusion

The more an individual says 'No' to sin and 'Yes' to the Lord's direction, the more he grows in the faith.

Prayer Points

1. Thanks for how far you have taken me in the faith.
2. For all my life I have followed and focused on human beings. Teach me how to focus on Jesus Christ, the author and finisher of my faith.
3. Enable me to always say 'No' to sin, and 'Yes' to God.

4. Deliver me from my commitment to self and the flesh.
5. Holy Spirit, help me to develop an intercessory prayer life.
6. Make me a vessel of honour in your service oh God!

Adult (Matured) Believers (Perfection)

Text: Hebrews 6:1-12

Memory Verse: 1 Corinthians 4:1-3

Introduction

When a believer is committed to the principles stated in study 2&3 above, it is definite that in a matter of a short while, he would be reckoned both in heaven and on earth as a grown (adult) believer.

Since the word 'adult' is a simple English word, it should not be difficult to identify an adult believer. He is the one who would not complain when he needs to make sacrifice. When his needs or prayer requests are not met, he is not the type who will begrudge God.

He is the type who could give anything to God without anticipating a reward or celebrated for it.

He is the believer who knows his God so well that he could go on with God when everyone else or everything has failed. He knows his placement in God's work and is satisfied to do exactly that and make God happy.

Other Characteristics Of The Matured Believer

1. He understands and is committed to the broad subject and personal dimension of vision and not ambition. That is he knows his vision and understands the correlation between his own vision and the vision of the entire Church.
2. He is a steward of time, money and every resources of God at his disposal. When he gives to God, he does not imagine that he did God favour.
3. God conscious at all times.

4. He is a pilgrim who understands the brevity of his stay on earth and always expecting the Rapture at all times.
5. Sold out to soul winning. And would always be doing something about it daily.
6. He is trouble to the kingdom of darkness and a source of joy to heaven daily.
7. Always ready and eager to impart the knowledge of God to others, directly or indirectly by taking them to places where they would learn.
8. He is completely committed (would not stop at anything) to the expansion of God's kingdom.
9. God-pleaser and not man pleaser.
10. He understands the basic doctrines and principles of scriptures and would not trivialize or water them down. He could not easily be deceived or fooled by false doctrines and the false prophets.

11. He knows and remains fully committed to the principles of establishment in the faith.
12. Has victory or control over the flesh and his emotions: anger, sexual urge, etc.

Conclusion

It takes a lot of experience with God to get there.

Prayer Points

1. There is no other anchor but the Word of God.
   - Help me to develop a deep root into the Word.
2. Make me a better steward of time, money and other resources you have kept in my care.
3. Help me to always be conscious of You and your presence everywhere I go.

4. Saul lost his position because he was a man pleaser. And I know you hate men pleasers.
   - Help me to shift my attention, affection from men to You.
5. Help me to understand the principle of stewardship, from your perspective.
6. Teach me the deep doctrines of the scriptures, so I can teach others.
7. It is a shame that I have accepted Jesus for long, but I am just a burden to others. It is time for me to begin to bless others.

   -Give me the grace to become a blessing.

Have You Been Blessed?

I am excited that this book has blessed you.

Do you know you could support me to bless another person?

We have about 200 kids in The Answer Mission Nursery and Primary school, Ogundepo, Muslim, Ibadan; where tuition is free. It is our mission to our neighbourhood. You could give anything to support the school.

Call Rev. Joke Olowosoyo on +2348056257056.

Pay your gift to UBA Account No: 1007294845 for The Answer Bible Church or gbenga@olowosoyo.org on PayPal; or Olowosoyo@yahoo.com on Interac.

He who has pity on the poor lends to the LORD, And He will pay back what he has given. Proverbs 19:17

Other Books by the Same Author

That Same Jesus

Joshua's Promotion

A New Life

The Lord is My Shepherd

Pursuit of Excellence

Procure Honour

The Power of Relationship

Aborted Priesthood

Essence of Marriage

Finding a Spouse

A New Beginning

Spiritual Contentions

God Answers Prayers

You Can Be Rich

Responsibilities in the family

Legacy of Service

Receiving Grace through the Anointing

Furrows of the Stream (a novel)

Covenant of Son-ship

Arise and Shine

Making Right Choices

The Beauty of Obedience

The Honour of Representing God

The Honour of Servant-hood

The Sure Mercies of David

A Peculiar People

Running & Winning the Race

That Anger May Send You to Hell

The Honour of Belonging to God

Elizabeth's Error

The Greatest Error of my Life

Walking with God

Marriage Covenant 1-14

An Unforgettable Day

Walking in God's favour

God's Generals (a novel)

Short Stories

Keeping a Spouse

Immorality does not pay

Divorce

The Failed Mission

Witchcraft in Leadership

Servant Leadership

Spiritual Leadership

Discipleship

Danieli - Eko Bibeli (Yoruba)

Daniel – A Study Manual

New Creature – A Study Manual

Real Stories

Every Believer a Leader

Spiritual Warfare – A Study Manual

The Greatest Regret of my Life

What Did I Do Wrong?

Church Branches?

Receiving Ability through the Anointed

What a Shame

Ministerial Ethics 1

Tell Kola that I Am Sorry

When Leaders make mistakes

Establishment in Christ

Solomon – a Bible Study Manual

Living a Valuable Life

Jonah – the Rebellious Prophet

Haba! Pastor (A Novel)

Saul – a Bible Study Manual

The Fire of Sexual Emotions

www.ingramcontent.com/pod-product-compliance
Ingram Content Group UK Ltd.
Pitfield, Milton Keynes, MK11 3LW, UK
UKHW041904190726
13854UKWH00003B/1082